# Presidents' Day

By Sheri Dean

 **Gareth Stevens**
Publishing

Please visit our Web site, www.garethstevens.com. For a free color catalog of all our high-quality books, call toll free 1-800-542-2595 or fax 1-877-542-2596.

Library of Congress Cataloging-in-Publication Data

Dean, Sheri.
  Presidents' Day / Sheri Dean.
    p. cm. — (Our country's holidays)
  Includes index.
  ISBN 978-1-4339-3924-2 (pbk.)
  ISBN 978-1-4339-3925-9 (6-pack)
  ISBN 978-1-4339-3923-5 (library binding)
  1. Presidents' Day—Juvenile literature. 2. Presidents—United States—History—Juvenile literature. I. Title.
  E176.8.D44 2011
  394.261—dc22
                        2010001058

New edition published 2011 by
**Gareth Stevens Publishing**
111 East 14th Street, Suite 349
New York, NY 10003

New text and images this edition copyright © 2011 Gareth Stevens Publishing

Original edition published 2006 by Weekly Reader® Books
An imprint of Gareth Stevens Publishing
Original edition text and images copyright © 2006 Gareth Stevens Publishing

Art direction: Haley Harasymiw, Tammy Gruenwald
Page layout: Daniel Hosek, Katherine A. Goedheer
Editorial direction: Kerri O'Donnell, Diane Laska Swanke

Photo credits: Cover (both images), pp. 1 (both images), 11, 15, 17, back cover (both images) Shutterstock.com; p. 5 Darren McCollester/Getty Images; pp. 7, 9 Hulton Archive/Getty Images; p. 13 © Bob Daemmerich/PhotoEdit; p. 19 courtesy Library of Congress; p. 21 © Michael Newman/ PhotoEdit.

Printed in the United States of America

CPSIA compliance information: Batch #CS10GS: For further information contact Gareth Stevens, New York, New York at 1-800-542-2595.

# Table of Contents

What Is Presidents' Day? . . . . . . . . 4

Honoring Our Presidents . . . . . . . 10

A Future President . . . . . . . . . . . 20

Glossary. . . . . . . . . . . . . . . . . 22

For More Information. . . . . . . . . 23

Index . . . . . . . . . . . . . . . . . . . 24

**Boldface** words appear in the glossary.

## What Is Presidents' Day?

On Presidents' Day, we think about the president of our country. It is a day to think about all the presidents who have led our nation.

4

**President Barack Obama**

5

George Washington was our country's first president. He was born in Virginia on February 22, 1732. He helped found our country.

President George Washington

7

Abraham Lincoln was our country's sixteenth president. He was born on a Kentucky farm on February 12, 1809. He kept our country from breaking apart after the **Civil War**.

President Abraham Lincoln

9

## Honoring Our Presidents

Years ago, Washington and Lincoln were the only presidents we honored with **special** days. Today, we honor all our presidents on Presidents' Day.

# FEBRUARY

| Sunday | Monday | Tuesday | Wednesday | Thursday | Friday | Saturday |
|--------|--------|---------|-----------|----------|--------|----------|
|        |        | 1       | 2         | 3        | 4      | 5        |
| 6      | 7      | 8       | 9         | 10       | 11     | 12       |
| 13     | 14     | 15      | 16        | 17       | 18     | 19       |
| 20     | 21 Presidents' Day | 22 | 23 | 24 | 25 | 26 |
| 27     | 28     |         |           |          |        |          |

11

Presidents' Day is the third Monday in February. People remember what presidents have done for our country. Bands play music. Some people march in **parades**.

On Presidents' Day, people also visit the **memorials** of presidents who have died. Many people go to the Lincoln Memorial in **Washington, D.C.**

14

At school, we learn about the lives of the presidents. We read stories about them and write reports.

# George Washington

- first president of the United States
- general during Revolutionary War

Our country has had over 40 presidents. So far, all the presidents have been men. A woman can be president, too.

## A Future President

The president is the leader of our nation. That is a very important job. Would you like to be president? What would you do for our country?

# Glossary

**Civil War:** the war between the Northern and Southern states (1861–1865)

**memorial:** something that reminds us of a person who has died

**parade:** a special show of marching people and bands

**special:** important

**Washington, D.C.:** the city that is the capital of our country

# For More Information

## Books

McNamara, Margaret. *Presidents' Day*. New York, NY: Aladdin, 2010.

Peppas, Lynn. *Presidents' Day*. New York, NY: Crabtree Publishing Company, 2010.

## Web Sites

### Fireworks University: The History of Presidents' Day

*www.fireworks.com/holidays/Presidents-day.asp*
Read the history of Presidents' Day and learn fun facts about our presidents.

### Presidents' Day

*www.kidzworld.com/article/399-presidents-day*
Learn about the origin of the holiday and see a timeline of U.S. presidents.

# Index

bands 12

Civil War 8

country 4, 6, 8, 12, 18, 20

February 6, 8, 12

Kentucky 8

leader 20

Lincoln, Abraham 8, 9, 10

Lincoln Memorial 14

memorials 14

men 18

nation 4, 20

Obama, Barack 5

parades 12

school 16

Virginia 6

Washington, D.C. 14

Washington, George 6, 7, 10

woman 18

## About the Author

**Sheri Dean** is a school librarian in Milwaukee, Wisconsin. She was an elementary school teacher for 14 years. She enjoys introducing books and information to curious children and adults.

DISNEY LEARNING

Disney Coding Adventures

# Bugs and Errors with

DISNEY

WRECK-IT RALPH

Allyssa Loya

Lerner Publications ◆ Minneapolis

Lerner Publications Company
A division of Lerner Publishing Group, Inc.
241 First Avenue North
Minneapolis, MN 55401 USA

For reading levels and more information, look up this title at www.lernerbooks.com.

Additional graphics provided by Laura Westlund/Independent Picture Service.

Main body text set in Billy Infant Regular 14/20.
Typeface provided by SparkyType.

**Library of Congress Cataloging-in-Publication Data**

Names: Loya, Allyssa, author.
Title: Bugs and errors with Wreck-it Ralph / Allyssa Loya.
Description: Minneapolis, MN : Lerner Publications Company, [2018] | Series: Disney coding adventures | Includes bibliographical references and index. | Audience: Ages 6–9. | Audience: Grades K to 3.
Identifiers: LCCN 2018002323 (print) | LCCN 2018014085 (ebook) | ISBN 9781541524347 (eb pdf) | ISBN 9781541524316 (lb : alk. paper) | ISBN 9781541526778 (pb : alk. paper)
Subjects: LCSH: Computer algorithms—Juvenile literature. | Debugging in computer science—Juvenile literature. | Creative activities and seat work—Juvenile literature.
Classification: LCC QA76.9.A43 (ebook) | LCC QA76.9.A43 L6748 2018 (print) | DDC 005.1—dc23

LC record available at https://lccn.loc.gov/2018002323

Manufactured in the United States of America
1-44519-34769-4/10/2018

# Table of Contents

What Are Bugs and Errors? . . . . . . . . . . .4

Fix It, Felix!. . . . . . . . . . . . . . . . . . . . .6

Ralph Crashes the Party . . . . . . . . . . .8

*Hero's Duty* . . . . . . . . . . . . . . . . . . . 10

Double Stripe! . . . . . . . . . . . . . . . . . 12

Building a Kart . . . . . . . . . . . . . . . . . 14

Escape the Nesquik-Sand. . . . . . . . . 18

Learning to Drive. . . . . . . . . . . . . . . .20

Random Roster Race. . . . . . . . . . . . .22

Diet Cola Mountain . . . . . . . . . . . . . 24

Fixing *Sugar Rush* . . . . . . . . . . . . . .26

Keep Coding! . . . . . . . . . . . . . . . . . . 28

Answer Key . . . . . . . . . . . . . . . . . . . .30

Glossary . . . . . . . . . . . . . . . . . . . . . .30

Further Information . . . . . . . . . . . . . . .31

Index . . . . . . . . . . . . . . . . . . . . . . . .32

# What Are Bugs and Errors?

Computers are awesome! People use them every day to do work and have fun. Did you know that computers need algorithms to work? Algorithms are groups of instructions called code. They tell computers what to do.

Algorithms don't always work. They may have mistakes called bugs. For example, an algorithm to take two steps forward may look like this:

➡➡

Each arrow gives an instruction. The same algorithm with a bug looks like this:

➡⬅

Instead of two steps forward, the algorithm says to take one step forward and one step backward. The algorithm has a bug and must be fixed, or resolved.

*Wreck-It Ralph* characters get into lots of trouble during their adventures. You can use algorithms to help them! But an algorithm won't work if it has bugs. So, let's make sure your algorithms are bug-free! For some of these activities, you'll need a partner, plain paper, construction paper, scissors, and pencils.

# Fix It, Felix!

Fix-It Felix fixes everything. He needs to reach the window that Ralph wrecked.

Help Felix reach the broken window and learn about bugs at the same time! Look at the building on the next page. Do you see Felix on the lower-right side? Then look at the list of algorithms below the building. Choose the algorithm that will move Felix to the broken window. If an algorithm doesn't work, it has a bug.

a.

b.

c.

Check your answers on page 30.

# Ralph Crashes the Party

The Nicelanders are having a party. Ralph wants something to eat. Help him move across the room to the cake shaped like a building.

Look at the map on the next page. Pretend to be Ralph and run, or start, this algorithm:

➡➡➡➡➡⬆

START

END

Did you bump into people? If so, the algorithm has bugs. Decompose the problem. That means think about the steps that will get Ralph to the cake. Then write a new algorithm with arrows on your own paper. Avoid bumping into people or the couch. Go to page 30 to see one possible answer.

# Hero's Duty

Ralph won the Medal of Heroes! He needs to escape *Hero's Duty* without touching any cybug eggs.

Cut a sheet of construction paper into about twenty egg-shaped pieces. Pretend each piece is a cybug egg. Next, spread the eggs on the floor. Make at least one clear path through the eggs.

Then decompose the problem. On your own paper, write an algorithm to walk across the room without touching any cybug eggs. Use an arrow for each step.

Run the algorithm when you're ready. You should follow each step carefully. If you touch an egg, the algorithm has bugs. Resolve the bugs, and run the algorithm again.

# Double Stripe!

The Medal of Heroes is hanging from the top of a candy-cane tree. Ralph wants it back. Can he beat Vanellope to the top of the tree?

Ralph ran this algorithm to reach the medal:

⬆ ⬅ ⬅ ⬅ ⬆ ⬆ ⬆ ⬆ ➡

Those steps had bugs. They brought Ralph to a branch with double stripes. Double-striped branches disappear when Ralph touches them. Look at the trees. Think about a path that avoids double stripes. Then write an algorithm on your own paper that brings Ralph to the medal.

END

START

13

# Building a Kart

Ralph and Vanellope broke into the kart bakery. Help them build the kart of Vanellope's dreams.

Sometimes code tells a computer to repeat an action. Instead of writing the same instruction many times, you can use loops. Loops tell computers how many times to do the same thing.

Look at the grid on the next page. You could use this algorithm to move Ralph and Vanellope to the gummy worms and then the sprinkles:

Or you could use an algorithm with loops:

2(➡) 2(⬇)

The numbers tell a computer how many times to repeat an action. The loops are easier to write.

What sweet items would you pick if you made a kart? Make a list on your own paper of three sweets from the grid on page 17. Then give your list to a partner. Your partner will write an algorithm to move Ralph and Vanellope to each sweet. Make sure your partner uses loops! Run the algorithm together when your partner is finished. Does it work? If not, it has bugs. Resolve it and try again. When you're finished, switch and have your partner make the list of sweets.

START

#5

17

# Escape the Nesquik-Sand

Felix and Sergeant Calhoun are stuck in Nesquik-sand! If they can make the Laffy Taffy vines laugh, Felix and Calhoun can grab the vines and escape.

Think of ten of your favorite jokes. If you don't know ten jokes, check out a jokebook from the library. Then grab a stuffed animal, and find a partner.

Face your partner from five steps away. Your partner will pretend to be Laffy Taffy. You and the stuffed animal are Calhoun and Felix. It's time to make your partner laugh!

Think of each joke as a line of code. Read a joke out loud. Did your partner laugh? If so, your partner will take one step forward. If your partner didn't laugh, the joke has a bug. Move on to the next joke. Calhoun and Felix will be saved when Laffy Taffy laughs five times. And you'll have an algorithm of funny jokes with no bugs!

# Learning to Drive

Vanellope wants to race. She practices with Ralph inside Diet Cola Mountain.

Look at the paths on the next page. Vanellope can drive straight if the path is clear. But if there's a hole in the path, she must swerve to avoid it. Each hole should have a swerve symbol below it. If it doesn't, it has bugs.

Run the algorithm below each path. Did you find all the bugs?
Write new algorithms on your own paper that will get Vanellope
to the end of each path.

drive straight = ➡

swerve = 〰➡

# Random Roster Race

It's time for the Random Roster Race. Watch out for gumballs and ice-cream attacks!

Cut about twenty squares from construction paper. Make the squares the same size. Draw Vanellope on one square. Draw a finish line on another square. Set the two squares aside.

Next, draw ice-cream attacks on two blank squares. Put gumball attacks on two different squares. Turn over the four attack squares, and mix them with the blank squares. Lay all the squares facedown in a grid like the one on the next page. Make Vanellope the lower-left square. Put the Finish Line square in the upper right. Vanellope and the Finish Line should be facing up so you can see where they are.

Write an algorithm on plain paper to get Vanellope to the Finish Line. Remember to use looped lines of code. Run the algorithm, and turn the squares over one by one. If you run into a trap, that means your algorithm has a bug. Rewrite it to go around the bug. Keep going until your algorithm reaches the Finish Line.

# Diet Cola Mountain

Ralph's friends are trapped by cybugs! He can save them if he smashes the top of Diet Cola Mountain. But first, he needs to get up there.

Ralph can't climb with all these cybugs in the way. He needs to push away each cybug before he can do the next step. Ralph tried to follow this algorithm to climb the mountain:
2(⬆) 2(➡) 3(⬆) 3(push) 2(⬆) ➡ 2(push)

END

The algorithm has bugs, though. The steps are in the wrong order.

Look at the grid on this page. Then fix the algorithm. Change the order of the steps until it brings Ralph to the top of Diet Cola Mountain.

START

# Fixing *Sugar Rush*

The cybugs are gone! But they left behind a big mess. *Sugar Rush* needs to be fixed.

In this project, you and your partner will each draw a grid like the one on the next page. Draw Fix-It Felix in the upper-left square. Add Sour Bill to five of the squares. These are the places where the world of *Sugar Rush* is broken, or has errors. You can put Sour Bill anywhere.

Trade grids with your partner. Write an algorithm to move Fix-It Felix to each square where Sour Bill appears on your partner's grid. Use Felix's hammer to fix each error. For example, this algorithm could fix the grid on page 27:

⬇ 🔨 2(⬇) 🔨 2(➡) 🔨 3(⬆) 🔨 3(➡) 2(⬇) 🔨

Does your algorithm fix every square where Sour Bill appears on your partner's grid? If not, resolve the bugs in your algorithm and run it again.

# Keep Coding!

After learning about bugs and errors, you may start seeing them everywhere. Mistakes people make are like bugs. Think about mistakes you see in your daily life.

Was the school bus late in the morning? Did you trip walking up the steps? Did your pencil break? Did your friend drop some food during lunch?

When a mistake happens, think about algorithms. What steps led to the mistake? Was your shoelace untied? Maybe you pressed too hard on your pencil. Then think about how to fix the error and avoid the mistake in the future. Soon you'll be great at spotting and fixing bugs!

# Answer Key

Page 7: b

Page 9: ↑➡➡➡➡➡

Page 13: ↑↑↑↑←←←↑↑➡

Page 21:  ➡〰 ➡〰

➡〰 ➡〰〰 ➡

〰 ➡➡〰〰➡〰 ➡

Page 25: 2(↑) 2(push) 2(➡) 2(↑) 3(push) ➡ 3(↑)

# Glossary

**algorithm:** instructions, made up of lines of code, that tell a computer how to solve a problem or finish a job

**bug:** a mistake in lines of code

**code:** instructions that computers can follow

**decompose:** to take a big problem and break it down into small pieces to figure it out

**loop:** a line of code that tells a computer to repeat an instruction a certain number of times

**resolve:** fix a mistake (a bug) in a line of code

**run:** to start an algorithm

# Further Information

CodeMonkey
https://www.playcodemonkey.com

Code.org
https://code.org/learn

Kelly, James F. *The Story of Coding*. New York: DK, 2017.

Lyons, Heather, and Elizabeth Tweedale. *Coding, Bugs, and Fixes*. Minneapolis: Lerner Publications, 2017.

Prottsman, Kiki. *My First Coding Book*. New York: DK, 2017.

# Index

algorithms, 4-6, 8-12, 14, 16,
   19, 21, 23-27, 29
arrows, 4, 9-10

decompose, 9-10

instructions, 4, 14

loops, 14, 16, 23

# About the Author

Allyssa Loya is an elementary school librarian in North Texas. Her passion for bringing meaningful learning to students led her to cultivate a technology-forward library that includes a makerspace and a coding club. While running the coding club in the library, she realized how important it is for every student to experience coding. Not every student will grow up to be a computer programmer, but all students will need to know how to think clearly and critically when they are adults.

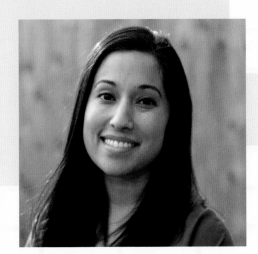

Loya is married to an IT manager, who is a perfect support system for her technological endeavors. Her two young boys are a constant reminder of the experiences that all students deserve from their educators.